# IMAGES OF ERIN

## IN THE AGE OF PARNELL

Published by the National Library of Ireland, 2000




British Library Cataloguing in Publication information available

ISBN 0 907328 34 2

Designed by Creative Inputs
Printed by Nicholson & Bass

# IMAGES OF ERIN

## IN THE AGE OF PARNELL

FROM THE COLLECTIONS OF
THE NATIONAL LIBRARY OF IRELAND

BY
L. PERRY CURTIS JR.

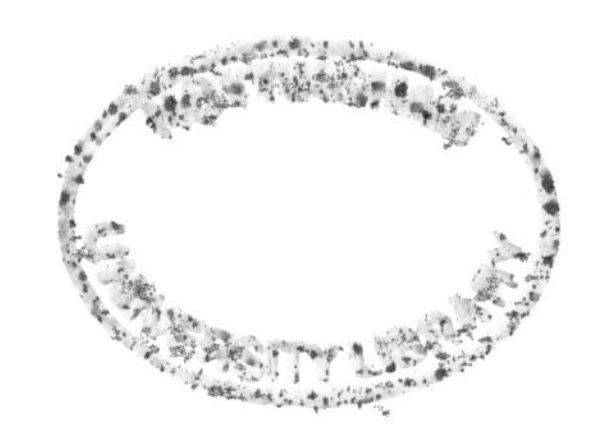

NATIONAL LIBRARY OF IRELAND

# CONTENTS

## List of Figures

## Acknowledgments

Thanks to the Beinecke Rare Book and Manuscript Library, Yale University, for illustrations from *Fun;* to the Baker Library, Dartmouth College for *The Irish "Vampire"*, and to the John Hay Library, Brown University, for *The Irish "Tempest"*.

Special thanks go forth to the Director of the National Library of Ireland, Mr. Brendan O'Donoghue, whose sponsorship and support for the exhibition have been invaluable. Also, Colette O'Daly, former Assistant Keeper of the Department of Prints and Drawings, has been the guardian angel of this project from the outset. Her encouragement and attention to all the details have earned my lasting gratitude. I am also indebted to her successor, Joanna Finegan, and to Avice-Claire McGovern, for their meticulous work in compiling the captions of the cartoons on display and assembling the illustrations for this book. Thanks also to Catherine Fahy, Assistant Keeper, and to John Farrell, for their help in producing this book and the associated exhibition. Last but not least, both Jim Scully and Kevin Browne deserve thanks for all their faith and good works in the National Library over the years.

## Foreword

The Prints and Drawings Department in the National Library of Ireland contains a wide variety of material, often unexpected and always interesting. Among the most colourful collections are the late nineteenth century cartoons that are the subject matter of this book. Professor L. Perry Curtis Jr. has provided us with a fascinating exposition on the theme of Erin as she appears in these cartoons and, indeed, a wonderful introduction to the collection as a whole. We are delighted to publish this book, in conjunction with an exhibition of the cartoons in the Library, beginning in October, 2000. Our thanks to Perry Curtis and congratulations on his exciting and innovative work.

**Brendan O'Donoghue**

Director, National Library of Ireland.

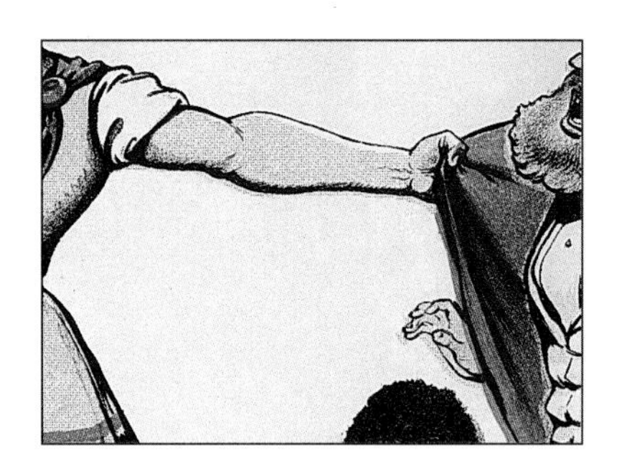

## Introduction

Thirty years ago the late Michael Hewson, then Keeper of Prints and Drawings (later Director) of the National Library of Ireland, kindly took me into one of the inner recesses of the library where he pulled open drawer after drawer filled with political cartoons dating from the 1870s and 1880s. This was my first glimpse of the treasures stored there and they seemed to invite 'discovery' by anyone with an interest in both Irish nationalism and political cartoons. Given the talents of comic artists like John Fergus O'Hea, John D. Reigh, and Thomas Fitzpatrick this combination of popular politics and art proved irresistible. By then my work on English images of the Irish in both literary and graphic form had reached the point of fascination with Irish responses to the steady stream of derogatory or denigrating stereotypes emanating from London - most vividly expressed by the cartoonists's transformation of militant Irish nationalists, especially Fenian or republican rebels, into apelike or bestial creatures.

The graphic 'simianization' of Paddy, the stereotypical Irish Catholic peasant rebel, became a vital part of the British imperial process that reinscribed in Anglo-Saxon eyes the necessity of imposing more repressive measures and stricter surveillance of political activity all over the country by the Royal Irish Constabulary and officials in Dublin Castle. To this ambitious political and cultural project, otherwise known as appropriating the colonized 'Other,' the artists and writers of *Punch, Fun, Judy*, and other London comic weeklies made their signal contributions. The memorable image of Paddy the apeman - marked indelibly by the sloping forehead, flaring nostrils, bulbous upper lip, and prognathous jaw of a chimpanzee or gorilla - sailed across the Atlantic and landed in comic weeklies from New York (*Judge* and *Puck*) to San Francisco (*The Wasp*). The cartoons or caricatures in the National Library contained ample proof that the Irish counterparts of Leech, Tenniel, Boucher, Sambourne, and others were not only aware of this

demonizing project but more than capable of replying to the nation's critics through the the medium of the new colour supplements or chromolithographs published every week in the *Weekly Freeman* and *United Ireland,* wherein they exposed the deliberate distortions of London's cartoonists and turned the tables on their detractors.

Out of my work on Anglo-Saxonist images of Paddy and Pat (*Apes and Angels,* Washington, D.C., 1971, 1997) grew an interest in other kinds of images and iconography - especially the reliance of Irish cartoonists on Erin or Hibernia as the feminine embodiment of both Parnellism and the emergent political nation. They used this immensely appealing icon to express not only 'the imagined community' of the Gaelic nation but also the militant brand of nationalism that emerged in 1878-9 as a result of the New Departure that forged a working alliance between those two closely related movements, Home Rule and tenant right or 'the land for the people'.

Further research in the Department of Prints and Drawings soon made me aware that Irish cartoonists had assigned more than one role to this comely maiden, who epitomized all that was most pure and noble, as well as Gaelic, about Ireland before the arrival of Strongbow and his Anglo-Norman-Welsh warriors. Contrary to the still conventional interpretation that comic artists cast Erin only as a mournful 'Mother Ireland' figure, who spent all her time in chains weeping over the deaths of her sons and daughters at the hands of British soldiers, wicked Anglo-Irish landlords, and cruel English politicians, I soon discovered that these (male) cartoonists greatly preferred the image of a beautiful young maiden, unencumbered by husband and children (of course all the Irish people were her family), who was both strong and infinitely desirable. In short, she was a far cry from the old hag or helpless woman - the Shan Van Vocht - who could only keen or cry 'ochone, ochone' and concede defeat. Although grieving and enchained Erins at the mercy of British coercion continued to appear in these cartoons, artists were fonder of depicting Erin as a young woman of great courage

and resolve, who could use both her feminine wiles and strength of will to lead the Irish people out of bondage and towards the promised land of independence.

Thus the dominant image of Erin conveyed in these amusing and yet melodramatic cartoons reflected the new confidence of a people committed to reinventing a pre-conquest identity as part of the collective enterprise known as nation-making. While the Celtic revival was slowly gathering momentum even before the fall of Parnell, Dublin's cartoonists and their viewers took great pride in not only Ireland's cultural heritage but also the palpable presence of 86 Irish Home Rulers in the imperial parliament at Westminster, led by the formidable Charles Stewart Parnell. These cultural and political developments, which were at times quite inseparable, reinforced the hope that the great goal of independence, conveyed time and again in these cartoons, lay just a few years ahead - especially after William Gladstone had completed his conversion to Home Rule in 1886. The arduous and costly campaigns fought by the Land League and the Parnellite National League during the 1880s required the support of the media; and in their own special way talented cartoonists like O'Hea, Reigh, and Fitzpatrick produced a striking form of propaganda that not only enhanced Erin's intrinsic appeal but also heightened the public's awareness of British wrongs and Irish rights.

L. Perry Curtis Jr., September 2000

# IMAGES OF ERIN IN THE AGE OF PARNELL

L. PERRY CURTIS, JR.

Although the iconic figure of Erin or Hibernia has a long history, the golden age of graphic images of this beautiful, young, and virtuous epitome of Ireland really belongs to the last third of the nineteenth century, when a number of talented Irish artists and illustrators emerged in Dublin. Of course, there was nothing new about the use of this romantic figure whether for political, commercial, or memorial purposes. For years, serious as well as comic artists all over Europe as well as in North America had been using the icon of a comely young woman to epitomize the nation in all its presumed purity, virtue, and valour. In 1830 the French romantic painter, Eugene Delacroix, produced his famous expression of a freedom-loving people rising up to defend their inalienable rights in *Liberty leading the people*: led by a beautiful, bare-breasted and musket-wielding young woman, the armed citizens of Paris are on their way to battle the authorities.

During the nineteenth century this alluring figure also symbolized every worthy cause, from freedom, democracy, temperance, truth, and justice to the socialist struggle for a workers' republic. In Ireland the image known as Hibernia or Erin also reminded viewers about the uniqueness of Irish identity by implying the existence of a purely Gaelic nation before the coming of the Anglo-Norman conquerors in 1169. This appealing image adorned every kind of artefact including commercial cards, china, silverware, harps and monuments or memorials honouring the heroes and martyrs of the long struggle for independence from Brian Boru to Wolfe Tone and beyond. The centenary celebrations of '1798' inspired a number of heroic male icons celebrating the sacrifice of so many thousands of United Irishmen during that bloody insurrection. By contrast the abortive Fenian uprising of the mid-1860s, especially the hanging of the three 'Manchester martyrs' in November 1867, gave rise to a number of commemorative Erins

perched on the tops of columns or pedestals in towns around the country. And, as Judith Hill points out in her recent study, *Irish Public Sculpture* (pp.114-32), the monumental and conflated figure of Erin and Liberty, bearing a harp or shield, enhanced public squares at the turn of the century. In England, however, comic artists were not always so kind or flattering when depicting Ireland's beloved icon. Thus a cartoon by William Dent of London in 1784, entitled 'Hibernia In the Character of Charity', revealed a plain-looking but smiling Hibernia seated on a kneeling and none-too-happy Britannia while breast-feeding the pigmy-sized politicians, Charles James Fox and Lord North.

The Irish origins of this iconic figure may be traced back to ancient myths and legends about powerful female warriors or goddesses, who littered the blood-stained soil with the bodies of their victims. Well-endowed with ample muscles and curves, these viragos loved to seduce and then kill the heroic male warriors they encountered on the battlefield or in the lists of love, especially those who dared to spurn their embraces. These Amazonian women made war and love with equal zest. Thus Medb (Maeve), Queen of Connacht, the prima donna of the great Ulster Cycle, the *Táin Bó Cuailgne* (the Cattle Raid of Cooley), could outrun a horse, change into various animals, and exhaust dozens of lovers. Along with her cuckholded husband, Ailill, she started the costly war against Ulster in order to possess the huge brown bull owned by the Herculean warrior, Cuchulainn. After he rebuffed her advances, she arranged his slow death in combat. Transformed into a raven, she perched on his shoulder while he bled to death defending himself against his foes.

During the seventeenth century a far more feminine and non-lethal icon emerged in the form of a maidenly figure embellishing the forepillar of a harp and appearing on coins minted in England and Ireland. Later she took her place on Ireland's official coat of arms. As rendered by artists of the romantic school, she was demure, pure, and always desirable. In

short, she possessed all the qualities associated with male fantasies of the ideal wife or lover for whom any true patriot should be prepared to die. Artists committed to the cause of Irish independence often drew on both pagan and Christian imagery in creating the feminized image of a once 'virgin' land before the conquest by the Gall or stranger. This epitome of Gaelic virtue and beauty combined the strength and valour of the warrior-goddess with the compassion of the faithful wife, mother, or sister. Part freedom fighter and part vestal virgin, she became the cherished icon of the Volunteers in the age of Grattan and also of the United Irishmen in the 1790s. Serving as a primary symbol of political resistance, Hibernia or Erin graced many a banner as well as the mastheads of newspapers promoting liberty, equality, and fraternity.

Following the Act of Union in 1800, Erin came to represent a colonized nation yearning to escape the yoke of John Bull. Despite all the literary allusions to 'Mother Ireland' the political cartoonists of Dublin deliberately chose to allegorize the nation as a nubile maiden unencumbered by children or husband and exposed to all the dangers arising out of the centuries-old fight for freedom. As Luke Gibbons has noted perceptively *(Transformations in Irish Culture, p.20)*, this visual allegory was 'not just a poetic device, but a figural practice that infiltrates everyday experience, giving rise to an aesthetics of the actual'. In the hands of nationalist artists then, almost all these images of Erin were closely connected to immediate political realities. Resonating with aspirations of both independence and a distinctly Gaelic identity, this appealing figure helped to invigorate the discourse of nationalism and sustain the morale of its votaries during the dark years of famine, starvation, eviction, heavy emigration, and coercion. After the famine, iconic Erin attained much wider circulation through the rapid expansion of newspapers and circulation figures. During the 1870s several Dublin papers embarked on a significant innovation by publishing a weekly or Sunday 'supplement' consisting of a cartoon-like insert that occupied a single or double page. The subject matter of this

cartoon resembled the so-called 'Big Cut' or 'Senior Cartoon' in *Punch* by fastening on political issues familiar to readers of the daily paper. Lacking any equivalent in the British press, these chromolithographs used four or five colours, which added much to their appeal. This new departure in newspaper content gave a filip to the *Weekly Freeman,* which pioneered the colour supplement for the additional price of 'three half-pence'. By 1879 these cartoons had grown bigger and bolder and contained brighter colours as well as better draughtsmanship. A few Dublin papers inserted them into their Saturday editions. Indeed, any reader with a shilling or two to spare could have a favourite cartoon framed and hung on the wall. Foremost among the papers that emulated the *Weekly Freeman* in this respect was *United Ireland,* launched by Parnell under the editorship of William O'Brien in 1881, which gave the colour supplement away free.

Needless to say these cartoons were an artful form of propaganda - a non-verbal or graphic editorial - designed to advance the cause of Parnellism and the Land League. Apart from the Christmas issue, the specific subject matter usually depended on the latest bone of Irish contention among politicians at Westminster or in Ireland. For weeks on end the principal focus might fall on the latest round of British coercion that was sending Land League or Home Rule activists to jail. In such cases the cartoons would be filled with demonic images of the red-bearded Irish Viceroy, Earl Spencer, or one of the more coercion-minded Chief Secretaries - William ('Buckshot') Forster or Arthur ('Bloody') Balfour. By the same token the cartoonist might hail Gladstone's conversion to Home Rule in 1886 or the return of John Dillon from a fund-raising trip overseas.

Appearing in roughly one third of all the colour supplements published in these two papers during the last twenty years of the century, Erin played a significant role in the propaganda war against unionism and landlordism, And she proved a versatile actor by playing a number of leading roles. Boasting an immediate appeal that no long-winded editorial could hope to

match, these cartoons were worth at least five thousand words - give or take the length of the captions accompanying them. Dublin's comic artists placed Erin in various melodramatic scenarios so as to highlight the oppressive nature of British rule and reinforce the solidarity of the Home Rule movement. In short these cartoons were designed to keep the flock faithful to the twin goals of independence and the abolition of landlordism.

The multiplicity of Erin's roles must be emphasized because some historians and cultural critics have reduced her iconic function to one of 'surrender and helplessness'. Thus, the opening footage of the semi-documentary film, *Mother Ireland* (1988), emphasizes the motif of defeat or abject despair. She has been constructed as the eternal maternal victim or mourner, drained of all her legendary strength and vitality during "the dark period" of the penal laws. The directors of this influential film cast her as the epitome of a colonized people who has abandoned all hope of ever being rescued by a brave (Stuart) prince coming across the seas from the Continent. Ignoring the crucial slippage between Mother and Daughter Ireland, the film-makers chose images of a young and vulnerable woman devoid of any ability to resist the tyranny of British cabinet ministers, Britannia, or John Bull. However, the frail and maidenly icon that appears in the selected cartoons does not fit the mould of the mature and motherly Dark Rosaleen, Cathleen Ní Houlihan, or the Shan Van Vocht (literally, poor old woman). Bound, chained, or gagged, this young woman lies helpless at the feet of Dublin Castle officials and rack-renting landlords. As we will see, many nationalist cartoons did indeed depict Erin at the mercy of such foes. But this was only one of the images employed by nationalist cartoonists to advance the cause of Home Rule. An equally favourite figure was that of a strong and defiant Erin endowed with all the power and the glory of Saint Joan of Arc. If she could never match Amazonian Britannia in physical or political, let alone military, strength, she was far from being the helpless victim of perfidious Albion

## The Five Faces of Erin

To appreciate the variety of roles played by Erin in these colour supplements during the heyday of Parnell it is necessary to sort out the hundreds of cartoons in which she appeared according to the specific scenario and the posture of the heroine, granted that the boundaries between one category and another are at best ambiguous or porous. In other words they are not carved in stone or cast in bronze simply because the history of art always entails subjective interpretation. So much depends on the eye or the sensibility of the beholder. For this reason it becomes the duty, indeed challenge, of every viewer to judge for himself/herself whether or not Erin's representation in any given cartoon properly belongs in the category assigned here. The five archetypes chosen fall under the following headings: Monumental, Enchained, Empowered, Courting, and Ambiguous. No doubt more precise or refined labels might be devised, but these five categories should help us to recognize the versatility of this icon as well as the lively imaginations of the artists who produced such striking images every week throughout the turbulent decade of Parnell's ascendancy.

## 1. Monumental Erin

Under the heading of 'Monumental' appears a regal yet passive figure who represents the dignity or majesty of the nation without lifting a hand to alter the status quo. Embroidered on a flag, imprinted on a card, frozen in glaze, or carved in stone as a memorial to the heroes of the long fight for independence, she stands or sits impassively surrounded by her loyal subjects and looking outwards with a calm and steady gaze. Neither defiant nor submissive but full of self-confidence, she represents a nation determined to assert its political equality with England within an imperial framework akin to Edmund Burke's ideal of liberty and authority. Occasionally depicted as the younger sister of Britannia, Erin appeared as the icon of Liberty on the balustrades of public buildings as well as atop memorials to the martyrs of past rebellions. Clad in a loose robe or dress and holding a harp, she exuded an aura of prosperity, peace, and national unity.

A classic example of monumental Hibernia, as she was known in the more Latinate era of Grattan, is the print produced by the Waterford-born artist, William Hincks, *Hibernia attended by her Brave Volunteers - EXHIBITING Her Commercial FREEDOM (c.1780)*, **Fig 1**. Hailing the legislative independence won by the Patriots in 1782, Hincks endowed her with majesty as she holds the banner of "Free Trade" above her head while standing on the shore of Dublin Bay filled with merchant ships. Guarded by two Volunteers, she accepts gifts or tributes from an American Indian and a Black man kneeling in supplication as if to emphasize the global nature of her mercantile interests. Much the same regal figure appears in the marble statue executed by John Hogan, entitled 'Cloncurry & Hibernia' (c.1846). Here iconic Erin holds the top of a harp while her left arm curves around the bust of Valentine Lawless, 2nd Baron Cloncurry and one foot rests on a recumbent wolfhound. John Henry Foley's famous bronze and stone memorial to Daniel O'Connell in the centre of Dublin's

**Fig 1**. William Hincks, *Hibernia attended by her Brave Volunteers EXHIBITING her Commercial FREEDOM* (n.d. c., 1780)

O'Connell Street contains a similar image of Hibernia standing next to other allegorical figures with her right arm extended and her hand pointing upwards to the Liberator at the summit. A symbol of national unity and commercial freedom, Erin also decorated many a Volunteer banner, flag, and medal during the 1780s. Both the Society of United Irishmen in the latter 1790s and Young Ireland in the early 1840s employed this same icon to advance their causes. At the same time, tradesmen or company directors had her features imprinted on trade cards and flyers advertising their services or wares. Thus Henry Brocas Senior's design for a Dublin insurance company featured Hibernia sitting in front of a truncated column bearing the address in College Green of the National Assurance Company, **Fig 2**. With her arm resting on a harp she is flanked by a document filled cornucopia and an anchor and fiery brazier. In the background several men direct a stream of water from a mobile pump at a building engulfed in flames.

From the late 1870s to the 1890s three of Ireland's most accomplished graphic artists - John Fergus O'Hea (c.1838-1922), John D. Reigh (fl. 1875-1914), and Thomas Fitzpatrick (1860-1912) - drew heavily on iconic Erin to convey the essence of an ecumenical Irish nationality. Well-known for their dedication to Home Rule, these political cartoonists also drew flattering chromolithographic portraits of the leading Parnellites at election times. Whatever the immediate political context, they endowed Erin with youth, femininity, and purity - not to mention bare feet. As befits the emblem of an all-Ireland

**Fig 2**. Henry Brocas Senior, Design for engraved card of the National Assurance Company of Ireland (n.d.)

movement, she transcended region, religion, class, and gender. Reminiscent at times of Princess Eva in Daniel Maclise's famous historical painting, *The Marriage of Strongbow and Eva* (1854), she also resembled the peasant girls in the paintings of Frederick William Burton as well as Thomas A. Jones's *Molly Macree* (1860) and Augustus Burke's *The Connemara Girl* (c.1880). Dark-haired with rounded facial features, she often wore a green-tinged tunic or cloak and rarely carried any weapon.

Although many of his cartoons were unsigned, O'Hea did use the penname SPEX. After moving from one comic weekly to another, he collaborated with Fitzpatrick on the staff of *Pat* during the early 1880s. Then the *Freeman's Journal* hired him to do the weekly cartoon for the Sunday edition. The equally talented Reigh drew for *Zoz* as well as *United Ireland* in the same decade. Harking back at times to the monumental Hibernias of the Hanoverian era, both artists celebrated the vicissitudes of a nation struggling to be reborn by means of Home Rule. Another monumental Erin appeared in O'Hea's *A Terrible Record* (*Weekly Freeman*, 2 July 1881), wherein she mourns the huge loss of some three million people since the great famine, **Fig 3**. O'Hea repeated this image in A *St. Patrick's Day Reflection* (*Weekly Freeman*, 17 March 1888) which reveals her lamenting the

**Fig 3**. J.F. O'Hea, *A Terrible Record* (*Weekly Freeman*, 2 July 1881)

population loss through famine and emigration. In *Soon !!!* (*Weekly Freeman*, 22 December 1888) she sits dejectedly while the spirit of Home Rule hovers over her shoulder, **Fig 4**. Inscribed on the wall behind her are the historic dates - 1798, 1829, 1848, 1867, and 1880 - signalling turning points in the nationalist struggle. One of O'Hea's finest variations on this theme was *Glasnevin* (*Weekly Freeman*, 11 October 1891), which appeared five days after Parnell's death, **Fig 5**. In this unsigned cartoon a grieving Erin lays a wreath inscribed 'There Be Peace' on the freshly-dug grave of the great leader. The message here implies that Parnell's moral lapse should not efface his contribution to the cause of independence and should certainly not be allowed to divide the nation into two warring camps.

**Fig 4**. O'Hea, *Soon !!!* (*Weekly Freeman*, 22 Dec.1888)

**Fig 5**. O'Hea, *Glasnevin* (*Weekly Freeman,* 11 Oct. 1891)

## 2. Enchained Erin

With this second category we enter a world of visual melodrama, wherein the cartoonists construct Erin as victim caught up in a mighty contest between the forces of good (Home Rule and the Land League) and those of evil (British rule and Irish landlordism). Here the artists left their audience in no doubt about all the obstacles that stood in the way of reaching the promised land. Under the heading of Enchained we find highly emotive images of Erin constantly subjugated or oppressed by 'the imperially male' power of Westminster. Scenarios in which Erin is bound in chains or tied to a stake by some malevolent and whip-wielding British viceroy or chief secretary proved one of the most enduring symbols in nationalist iconography. Ever so vulnerable, this Erin represents the classic female victim of a cruel or abusive John Bull and his agents of coercion. One can only imagine the appeal of this anti-imperial message to a public habituated to Crimes Acts or summary justice and deeply resentful over the imprisonment of its elected leaders for advocating self-government.

In *The "Land Bill" Mirage* (*Weekly Freeman,* 19 March 1881) O'Hea drew Erin manacled and stranded in an arid desert between two dead camels signifying 'The Constitution' and 'Liberty'. As two Liberal ministers thumb their noses while riding away on camels, she gazes at a mirage in the sky containing a prosperous farmhouse, abundant crops, and a scroll labeled 'Irish Land Bill', **Fig 6**. In a more forceful cartoon, *A Terrible Emergency* ! (*Weekly Freeman,* 24 December 1881), published at the height of Gladstonian coercion during the land war, Erin is bound by the belt of coercion while gorilla-like Orangemen and a wicked landlord flog her. This cartoon refers to the famous 'relief mission' composed of Orange Emergency men recruited in County Monaghan who were sent to Lough Mask under armed escort to harvest the crops of the boycotted Captain Boycott, **Fig 7**. Another version of hapless, helpless Erin appeared a week later. In *His Latest Triumph !* (*Weekly Freeman,* 31 December 1881),

**Fig 6**. O'Hea, *The "Land Bill" Mirage* (*Weekly Freeman*, 19 Mar. 1881)

**Fig 7**. O'Hea, *A Terrible Emergency !* (*Weekly Freeman*, 24 Dec. 1881)

a cruel and haughty Gladstone, dressed like St. George and riding a horse draped in the Union Jack, drags his victim along the ground, **Fig 8** .

During the spring of 1882, when Parnellite Members of Parliament were obstructing debate in Parliament and forcing Gladstone to curtail discussion by means of the cloture, O'Hea drew *At Their Mercy* (*Weekly Freeman,* 8 April 1882). Cast as a masked executioner, Gladstone stands over a gagged and bound Erin, who kneels and bows her head on the block of 'English Prejudice'. The axe held by the prime minister bears the words 'More Coercion', **Fig 9**.

**Fig 8**. O'Hea, *His Latest Triumph !* (*Weekly Freeman,* 31 Dec. 1881)

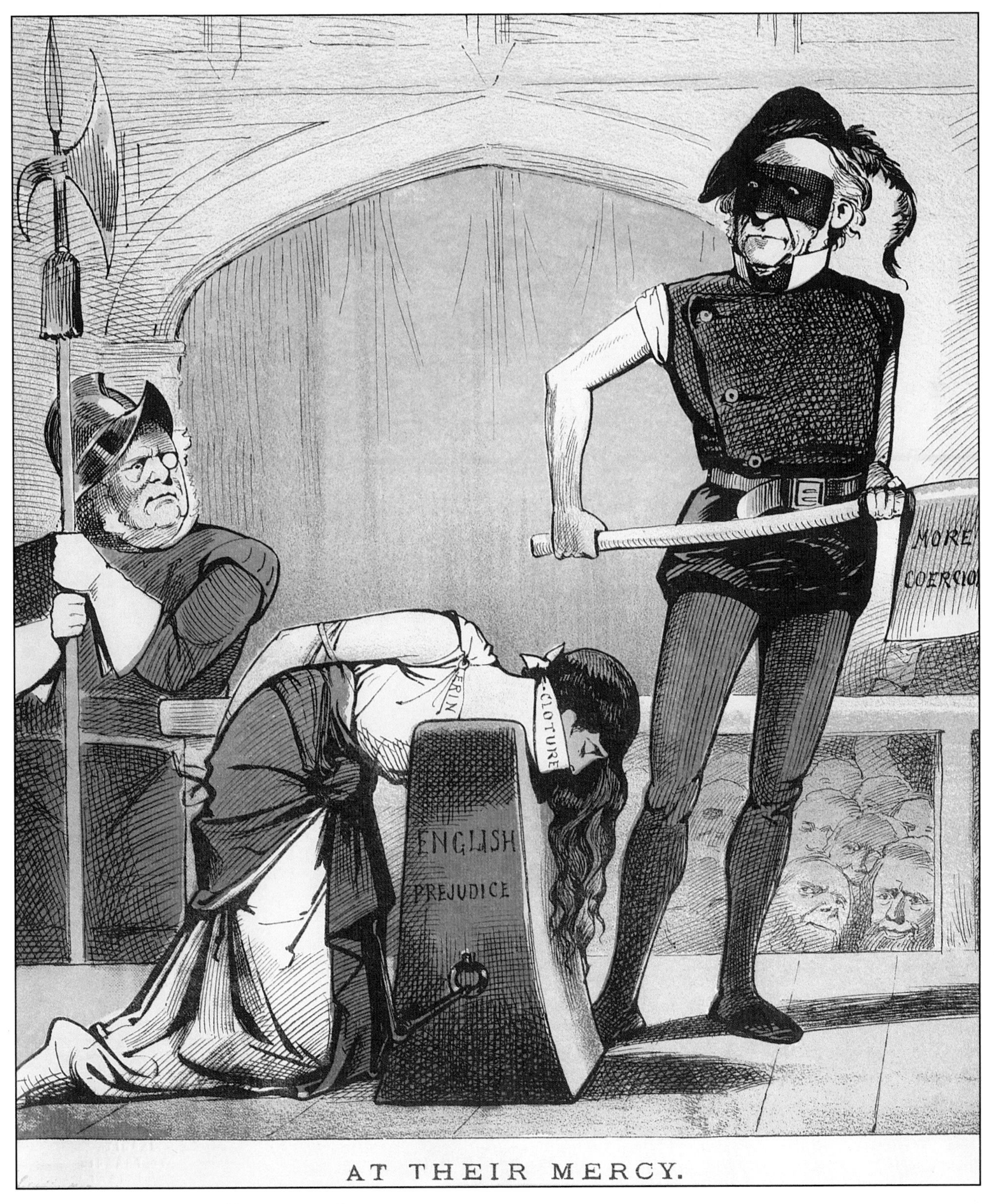


**Fig 9**. O'Hea, *At Their Mercy* (*Weekly Freeman*, 8 April 1882)

In *The Reason Why* (*Weekly Freeman*, 11 October 1884) Erin has been tied to a tree by coercive measures and faces two leering tormentors - the Tory leader, Lord Salisbury, and the Liberal prime minister, Gladstone, who are dressed as seventeenth-century bandits, **Fig 10**. In the rear a chivalric knight representing the new Franchise Bill rides to her rescue signifying more votes in favour of Home Rule.

Choosing an altogether different scenario just before the fall of Gladstone's administration, O'Hea produced *Doctors Differ* (*Weekly Freeman*, 16 May 1885). Here Erin lies on a sick bed covered in a tattered and torn Union Jack while three quack doctors - Joseph Chamberlain, Sir Charles Dilke, and the Viceroy, Lord Spencer - debate whether to treat her with the medicine of concession or a strong dose of coercion, **Fig 11**. Reprising the medical or surgical motif, O'Hea drew a helpless Erin just after the defeat of the first Home Rule Bill in 1886. In "On the *Dissecting Table*" - *Again* - *Perhaps* (*Weekly Freeman*, 31 July 1886), the leaders of the Unionist coalition - Lords Salisbury, Hartington, and Randolph Churchill along with Joe Chamberlain - sadistically prepare to dismember their patient, who is wrapped in a sheet labeled 'Tory Government', **Fig 12**.

**Fig 10**. O'Hea, *The Reason Why* (*Weekly Freeman*, 11 Oct 1884)

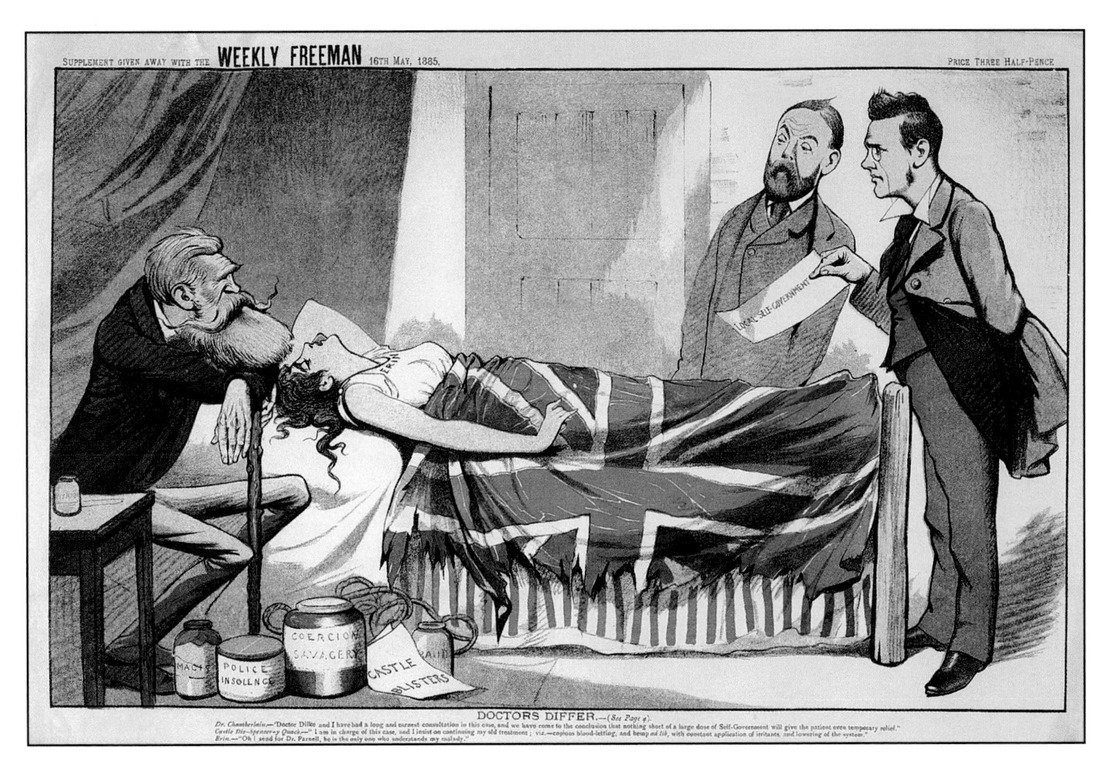


**Fig 11**. O'Hea, *Doctors Differ* (*Weekly Freeman*, 16 May 1885)

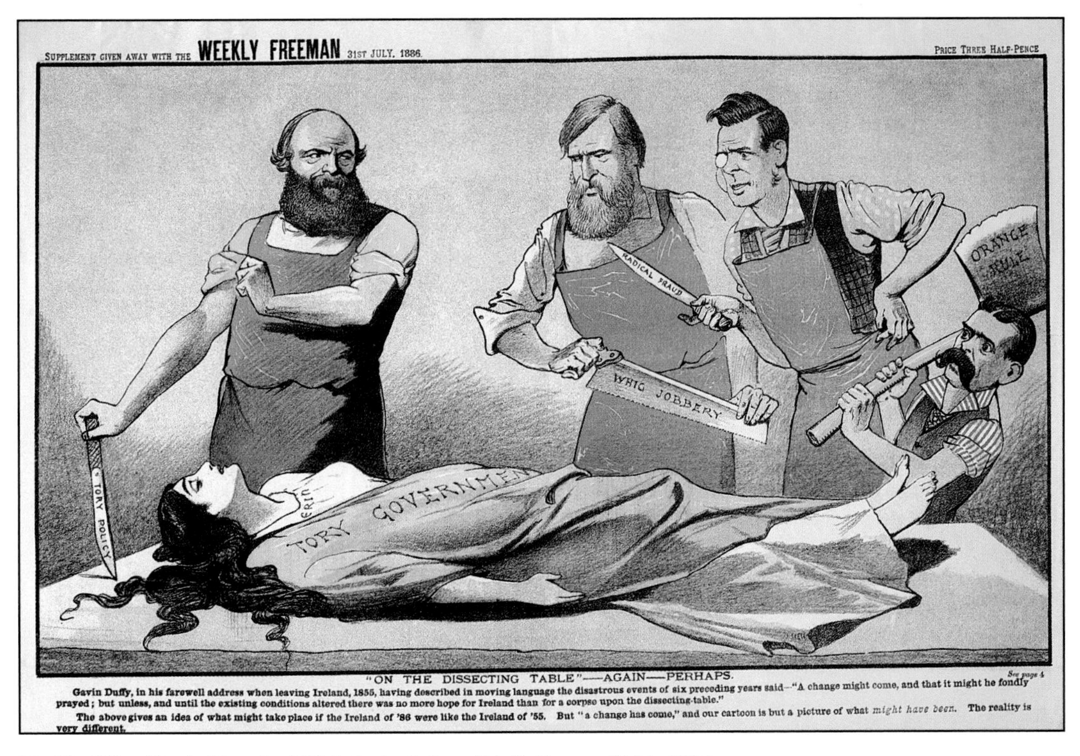


**Fig 12**. O'Hea, *"On the Dissecting Table" - Again - Perhaps* (*Weekly Freeman*, 31 July 1886)

"REJOICE, OH! GREATLY."

See page 4

Erin having deposited her Decoration at the Shrine of "LOYALTY" retires (on invitation) to an Imperial Institute to celebrate the Queen's Jubilee.

**Fig 13**. O'Hea, "*Rejoice, Oh ! Greatly*" (*Weekly Freeman*, 4 June 1887)

In 1887, just after the passage of the new stringent Crimes Act, O'Hea juxtaposed the joy of Queen Victoria's golden jubilee with the pain of Erin's imprisonment inside 'an Imperial Institute' in *"Rejoice, Oh ! Greatly"* (*Weekly Freeman,* 4 June 1887). Despite her declaration of 'Loyalty' she has been sent to cell number 87 by the stern governor (and prime minister), Lord Salisbury, who peers around the door at his prisoner as she points to the 'Jubilee Coercion Bill/Evictions/Closure/Poverty', **Fig 13**. More than a month later, while the new Chief Secretary, Arthur Balfour, was flexing his Unionist muscles with fresh measures of coercion, O'Hea drew *In The Lion's Den* (*Weekly Freeman,* 23 July 1887), **Fig 14**, which owed its existence to the romantic painting by the Prague-born artist, Gabriel Max (1840-1915), entitled *The Lion's Bride*. In both works a beautiful young woman lies on the floor of a lion's cage in a zoo as the ferocious beast prepares to devour his prey. But O'Hea has turned this exotic scenario into a political allegory. In his words, "Erin has been dragged into the Tory Den, but happily there is an 'ardent admirer' not far off". Her would-be deliverer is, of course, the Liberal convert to Home Rule, Gladstone, who stands just outside the cage holding the rifle of 'Democracy'. On the

**Fig 14**. O'Hea, *In The Lion's Den* (*Weekly Freeman,* 23 July 1887)

wall hangs a sign warning - 'The Lion "Tory" - Dangerous'. The following verses accompanied this cartoon: 'Alone in the den ! Is there no one to aid her? Shall her hopes thus be crushed? Is her last battle over? Have her allies deserted, forgotten, betrayed her?' Although supine on the floor, Erin clings to the green collar or crown of Home Rule.

In dealing with the Anglo-Irish conflict, some of London's best comic artists often invoked the classical myth of Andromeda, who was chained by her father to a sea-shore cliff as a sacrifice to appease the rage of the scaly sea-monster Cetus. She is spared this dreadful fate by Perseus, who rides to her rescue on his winged horse, Pegasus. In the hands of British cartoonists, the dragon represented Fenian rebels or republican dynamiters and assassins, while the Perseus-like deliverer of hapless Erin varied between Britannia, Gladstone, or an Irish viceroy determined to prosecute and punish political agitators who threatened her life or virtue. Thus in 1866 when the Fenian campaign was unnerving the British public, Tenniel produced *The Fenian-Pest* (*Punch,* 13 March 1866). Britannia appears here in the guise of Pallas Athena and rescues Erin from the clutches of a simianized Irish American Fenian. More than a decade later, at the height of the land war, Tenniel produced an equally imperious Britannia in *Two Forces* (*Punch,* 29 October 1881). Wielding the sword of 'The Law', she protects a cowering Hibernia from the ape-like figure menace of Irish 'Anarchy'. An all-suffering Erin or Hibernia also appeared in *The Irish "Tempest",* (*Punch,* 19 March 1870), wherein Tenniel allegorized Irish rebellion as a bestial Caliban named 'Rory of the Hills'. Armed to the teeth, this carnivorous gorilla lunges at Gladstone, who plays the part of Prospero protecting a frightened Miranda/Hibernia, **Fig 15**.

By contrast, Irish cartoonists usually cast Parnell in the role of Erin's rescuer. In *Jubilation and Desolation - Two Records,* drawn by Thomas Fitzpatrick (*Weekly Freeman,* (12 June 1897) during the Queen's diamond jubilee, a downcast Erin sits on the stone wall of a ruined cottage mourning the famines, evictions, emigration, and coercion that have afflicted her nation since Victoria first ascended the throne sixty years earlier. Standing above her is the consoling figure of Britannia with helmet and sheathed sword, who expresses sympathy for all of Ireland's suffering since 1837 including famine, eviction, and emigration. Significantly, she points out two British ironclad ships that are patrolling Ireland's waters offshore.

**Fig 15**. John Tenniel, The Irish "Tempest" (*Punch*, 19 March 1870)

## 3. Empowered Erin

A far different set of images appeared during the ascendancy of Parnell under the heading of Empowered. This iconic figure possessed all the strength and courage needed to defy the hereditary enemy and lead her people out of colonial subjection and towards the promised land of independence. Unconquerable and fearless, she could endure all the pain and suffering of British tyranny and defy anyone who threatened her virtue or freedom. After the launch of the New Departure in 1878, the founding of the Land League, and the emergence of Parnell as the dominant leader of the nationalist movement, Dublin's cartoonists produced a much more assertive, indeed, aggressive, Erin to inspire the cause. If this new-model icon lacked the bellicosity of Queen Medb or the ferocity of the Morrigan, she possessed great inner strength, loyalty, and courage along with youth and beauty. A veritable Joan of Arc wearing a white tunic overlain with a green mantle, she needed no armour or sword to lead her people. If she was unattached or single, there were strong hints of an engagement to her knight errant, Charles Stewart Parnell. Only on rare occasions did she ever appear as a mother shielding her children from British tyrants.

Refusing to back down before the bullying figure of John Bull, Empowered Erin managed to retain all the femininity of the two previous versions, if only because her creators shared the masculine tastes of the male-dominated Home Rule movement. In this respect she defied the Victorian rule that women could not be both feminine and powerful at the same time. Not unlike the image of the New Woman undergoing construction in England, especially in her yearning for independence and her indifference to marriage, this Erin was strong enough to defeat avaricious landlords, brutish Fenians, and coercive British politicians.

Singling out examples of this category for special mention is no simple task because so many of these exhortative images deserve discussion, not to mention illustration. We may begin with O'Hea's *"Avaunt and Quit My Sight"* (*Weekly Freeman*, 6 August 1881), wherein Erin firmly spurns the offer of a box of dynamite from the skeletal and hooded figure of the 'Spirit of Assassination', **Fig 16**. Holding a sheet of paper marked 'Argument', this emblem of constitutional protest stands in front of a large flag bearing the Parnellite motto, 'Legitimate Agitation'. A fortnight later O'Hea drew *"Remove That Bauble"* (*Weekly Freeman*, 20 August 1881), which appeared during the debate at Westminster over Gladstone's radical Irish Land Bill. Standing tall as the 'Spirit of the People' and wearing the cap of 'Democracy', she has invaded the House of Lords and is ordering a craven old peer to forsake the sceptre of 'Power' and pass the measure lying underneath the table, **Fig 17**. Gladstone looks on with mixed emotions as she cries out: "Begone". The large shillelagh in her right hand underscores her resolve not to be denied. In *Christmas 1884* (*Weekly Freeman*, 20 December 1884), SPEX or O'Hea drew Erin rising

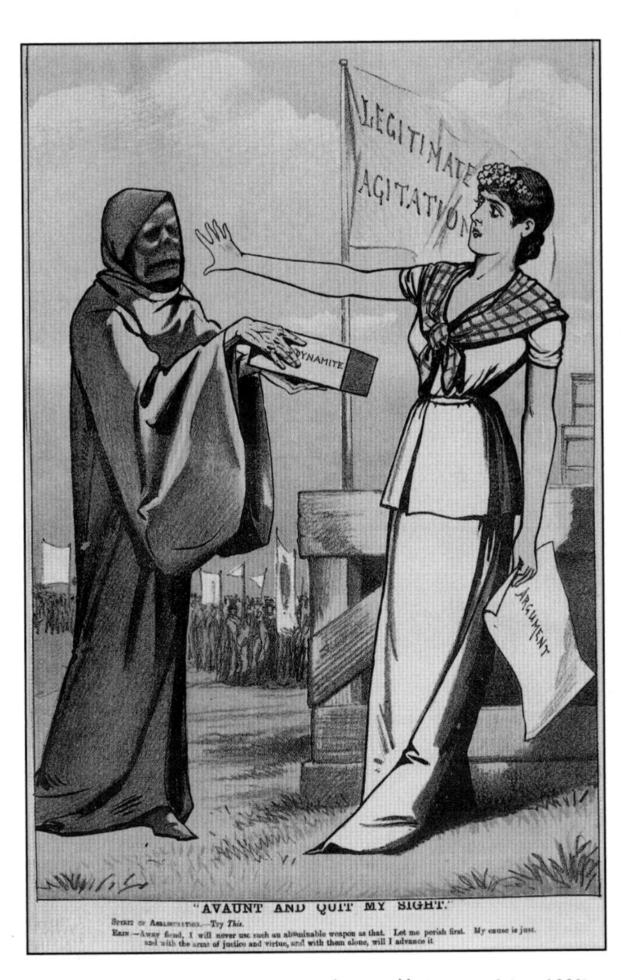


**Fig 16**. O'Hea, *"Avaunt and Quit My Sight"* (*Weekly Freeman*, 6 Aug. 1881)

**Fig 17**. O'Hea, *"Remove That Bauble"* (*Weekly Freeman*, 20 Aug. 1881)

triumphantly from a grave atop a snow-covered mountain while holding aloft a cross and the crown of Home Rule, **Fig 18**. The sun of freedom shines brightly on her flowing white dress. Inscribed on the tombstone in the rear are the words, 'Ireland Buried Here 1171', indicating the year of the arrival of the Norman king Henry II. In the foreground a fat John Bull cringes in fear and a broken flagstaff bearing the Union Jack lies on the ground. The red-bearded Viceroy, Lord Spencer, and his Chief Secretary seem equally awestruck by this resurrection. In O'Hea's *Breasting the Storm*, (*Weekly Freeman*, 23 January 1886), published while Gladstone was contemplating Home Rule, a fearless Erin stands barefoot on top of another rocky peak. Wearing a white dress with an orange-coloured cloak, she grasps the parchment of 'Constitutional Methods', **Fig 19**. With head held high she walks past a ferocious British lion and bulldog as well as a lethal serpent labeled 'Anti-Irish Press' coiled around a signpost marked 'To College Green'. Behind her flash bolts of lightning marked 'Martial Law', 'Coercion', and 'Extermination'. As the caption states, Erin is 'used to this sort of thing' and is resolved 'to reach my destination'.

**Fig 18**. O'Hea, *Christmas 1884* (*Weekly Freeman*, 20 Dec. 1884)

**Fig 19**. O'Hea, *Breasting the Storm* (*Weekly Freeman*, 23 Jan. 1886)

In November 1885 an unknown artist for the *Irish Pilot* replied with vigour to Tenniel's dramatic cartoon, *The Irish "Vampire"*, which had appeared in *Punch* on October 24, **Fig 20**. Tenniel gave his bloodthirsty bat the face of Parnell and inscribed on its wings the 'National League'. Hovering over a supine Hibernia in the predatory manner of Count Dracula, the vampire bat descends on his swooning victim with her throat exposed to his sharp fangs. In his reply, *The English Vampire* (7 November 1885), the Irish artist reversed Tenniel's imagery by drawing a powerful Erin wearing a white, orange, and green dress and warding off the evil bat of 'British Rule' with the shield of the 'National League' and a long sword, **Fig 21**.

A splendid example of Erin's strength appears in O'Hea's *Mad Dog !!!* (*Weekly Freeman*, 10 September 1887), wherein 'Miss Clare' wields the broom of 'Popular Determination' to chase away a little cur named Arthur Balfour, the Irish Chief Secretary, whose zeal for harsh repression earned him the epithet of 'Bloody Balfour'. Tied to the dog's tail is a kettle labelled 'Proclamation' - a reference to Balfour's fondness for imposing summary justice on districts deemed disturbed, **Fig 22**. O'Hea

**Fig 20**. John Tenniel, *The Irish "Vampire"* (*Punch*, 24 Oct. 1885)

**Fig 21.** Anon. *The English Vampire* (*Irish Pilot,* 7 Nov. 1885)

**Fig 22.** O'Hea, *Mad Dog !!!* (*Weekly Freeman,* 10 Sept. 1887)

also chose a whipping scene for *The Burning Question* (*Weekly Freeman*, 29 January 1887) which features Erin standing outside the House of Commons. Grasping the Irish Chief Secretary, Sir Michael Hicks Beach, by his lapel, she holds a cat-o'-nine-tails in her right hand poised to administer some lashes, **Fig 23**. Hicks Beach carries a large can of petrol destined for use in burning the cabins of evicted tenants on the Glenbeigh estate in County Kerry. In the background a stereotypically lean and mean landlord wearing a tattered 'pink' hunting coat raises his arms in protest. An equally empowered Erin appears in O'Hea's cartoon *Exorcising A Pest* (*Weekly Freeman*, 31 November 1883). Depicted as a dragon-slayer, she waves the flag of 'Nationality' and drives away the fire-breathing dragon of 'Orangeism,' while her daughter, Ulster, clings to her for protection, **Fig 24**. Reigh also created a powerful *Erin in Ireland Wrestles With Famine While Mr. Balfour Plays Golf* (*United Ireland*, 23 August 1890), which featured Erin grasping the spectre of famine while the Chief Secretary was enjoying his holiday in Scotland, **Fig 25**.

The bitter breakup of the Irish parliamentary party in the wake of the Kitty O'Shea divorce scandal in 1890 gave rise to a number of cartoons in which Erin lamented the split among her representatives and yearned for reconciliation. On this occasion Fitzpatrick produced *Erin Crushing The Serpent Faction* (*Weekly

**Fig 23.** O'Hea, *The Burning Question* (*Weekly Freeman*, 29 Jan. 1887)

**Fig 24**. O'Hea, *Exorcising a Pest* (*Weekly Freeman,* 31 Nov. 1883)

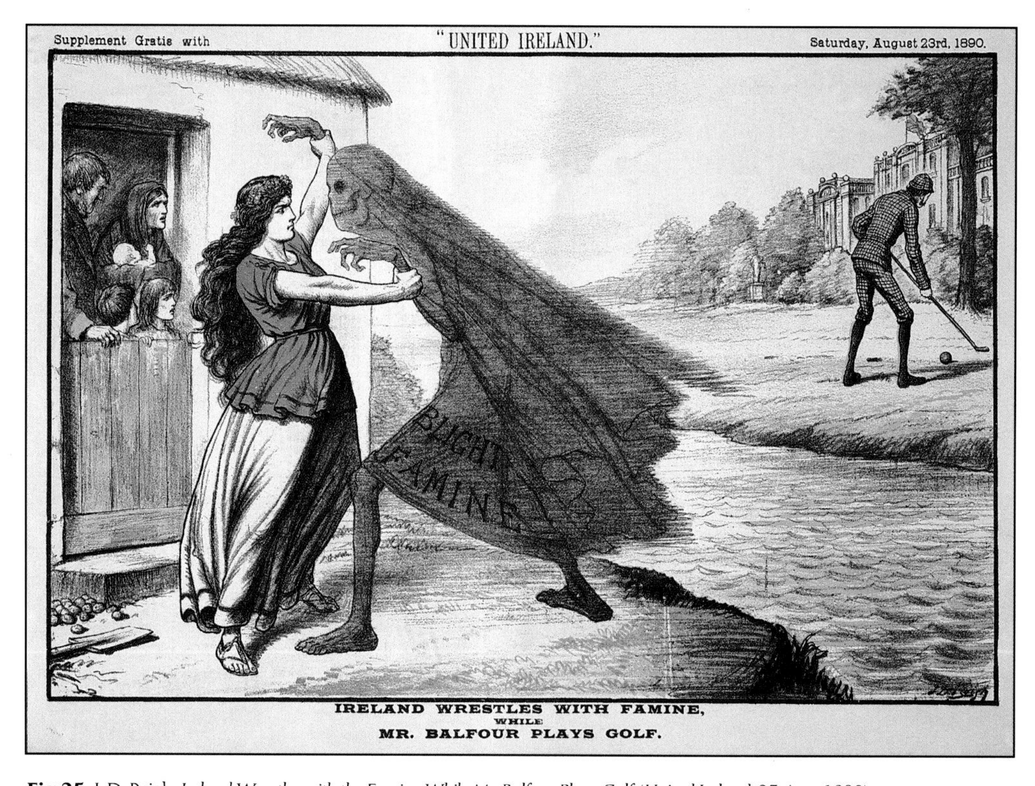


**Fig 25.** J. D. Reigh, *Ireland Wrestles with the Famine While Mr. Balfour Plays Golf* (*United Ireland,* 23 Aug. 1890)

*Freeman*, c1890-1) wherein a muscular Erin strangles the hydra of 'Faction' The three heads of this serpent belong to leading Parnellites (including John Redmond), whom the *Weekly Freeman* opposed. Last but not least, the commanding figure of Erin in O'Hea's *Immortal* (*Weekly Freeman*, 6 December 1890) stands atop a stone pillar with sword and treaty in hand. Behind her swirl the dark clouds of 'Disunion, Distraction, Passion, Treason' and 'Failure', **Fig 26**. Holding a sword and treaty, she observes solemnly: 'Men and parties may pass away, but I remain'. Published at the outset of the Parnellite party crisis arising out of the O'Shea divorce case, this cartoon articulates Erin's primary role as the muse or 'Spirit of Irish Nationality', who has the task of healing the wounds in the body politic.

Irish artists often used the serpent to symbolize Ireland's enemies including Irish-American Fenians. In an earlier version

**Fig 26**. O'Hea, *Immortal* (*Weekly Freeman*, 6 Dec. 1890)

of the reptilian motif, *Patriotism and Creed* (*The Pilot*, 31 October 1885), dedicated to Thomas Sexton, O'Hea drew a more spiritual but still strong Erin crushing the huge snake of 'English Atheism' beneath her feet. Gazing towards a shaft of sunlight labeled 'Dawn of Freedom', she carries a cross and green flag with a harp in the center. In 1891 O'Hea commemorated the 1798 rebellion in a far from comic cartoon, *A Scout of '98. "The Yeos' !!!"* (*Weekly Freeman*, 19 December 1891). Here a brave young woman, faintly reminiscent of Marianne but fully dressed in red skirt and white blouse, waves a red flag to warn her invisible United Irishmen comrades that the enemy (Yeomanry) approaches in the plain below, **Fig 27**. It would be hard to imagine a more heroic or historic use of this iconic figure in any of the colour supplements.

Needless to say, all the images of Empowered Erin anticipated the famous (unsigned) poster - *The Birth of the Irish Republic* - produced by Dublin's Art Depot after the Easter Rising in 1916, wherein a triumphant angel, symbolizing both war and peace, rises above a trench filled with rifle-firing Volunteers.

**Fig 27**. O'Hea, *Scout of '98. "The Yeos' !!!"* (*Weekly Freeman*, 19 Dec. 1891)

## 4. Courting Erin

The fourth category contains scenarios in which Erin is configured as not only the love object of British ministers but also a flirt or coquette who uses 'all those endearing young charms' to extract concessions from the government. On both sides of the Irish Sea cartoonists took delight in picturing her being wooed by Gladstone, Lord Salisbury or some other leading politician. At the same time she was quite capable of doing a little courting on her own account or rather on Ireland's behalf. Whereas English artists portrayed this Erin as a rather passive young woman being hassled or seduced by lustful British ministers, Irish cartoonists endowed her with the strength to keep them at arm's length while obtaining political favours. Thus she had no qualms about using her good looks to this end, while the leaders of the two main British parties, Gladstone and Salisbury, pursued her with other ideas in mind.

Some of the finest examples of courting Erin came from the drawing board of J. Gordon Thomson, the principal cartoonist of the British comic weekly *Fun*. In *John Bull's Valentine of Love and Reconciliation to Erin* (*Fun*, 16 February 1881), John Bull on bended knee holds Erin's hand while the Cupid-like figure of Gladstone flies overhead armed with his bow and quiver filled with the sharp arrows of coercion, **Fig 28**. Thomson assigned Gladstone the role of a troubadour wearing a dressing gown decorated with shamrocks in *Far from the Madding Crowd* (*Fun*, 5th December 1888). Here the Liberal leader cum Lothario serenades the almost alive bust of Erin on his banjo labeled 'Home Rule'. And the song he sings parodies Faust: 'They may wriggle, they may struggle, but I've got 'em in my eye; And I'll have 'em, yes I'll have 'em - I shall have 'em by-and-by !'.

St. Valentine's Day also inspired Dublin's cartoonists to put this lovers' festival to political use. Thus Reigh's *Erin's Valentine's*

**Fig 28**. J. G. Thomson, *John Bull's Valentine of Love and Reconciliation to Erin* (*Fun*, 16 Feb. 1881)

**Fig 29**. O'Hea, *Her New Valentine* (*Weekly Freeman,* 13 Feb. 1886)

*Compliments of the Season* (*United Ireland,* 16 February 1884) portrays Erin with her harp sitting amidst a profusion of Valentine cards signed by all the leading lights of the nationalist movement from O'Connell and the Fenians to the Parnellites. In her hand she grasps the fanciest card of all from Parnell, bearing the image of the Irish Parliament on College Green. In 1886, while Gladstone was putting the finishing touches on his Home Rule Bill, O'Hea cast him as Cupid in *Her New Valentine* (*Weekly Freeman,* 13 February 1886), **Fig 29**. Here the amorous prime minister aims an arrow at Erin, who is busy sewing the flag of legislative independence. The new Chief Secretary, John Morley, 'The Castle Mephistopheles', kneels before her with Valentine greetings in hand. But she shows no sign of succumbing to his blandishments. Thomson excelled at creating trysts between Erin and her suitors from Westminster. In *Asking His Intentions* (*Fun,* 24 February 1886), Gladstone carries a bouquet labeled 'Home Rule', while an unforgiving Mrs. John Bull demands to know exactly what his 'Intintions' are towards the beautiful Miss Erin, **Fig 30**.

In *'The Kissing and Hissing Game', As Played At St. Stephen's* (*Fun,* 24 March 1886), the venerable premier plants a kiss

FUN.—February 24, 1886.

ASKING HIS INTENTIONS.

*The O'Gladstone.*—"IS IT INTINTIONS THIN? SHURE, I'VE PLENTY OF 'EM, MRS. BULL; BUT JUST AT PRISINT I DON'T KNOW QUITE EXACTLY WHAT THEY ARE."

**Fig 30**. Thompson, *Asking His Intentions* (*Fun,* 24 Feb. 1886)

**Fig 31**. Thomson, *At The Irish Exhibition Hibernia and The Grand Old Masher* (*Fun,* 6 June 1888)

on Erin's cheek to the acute dismay of the Tory or Unionist leaders who hiss this new champion of Home Rule. And in one of Thomson's cleverest efforts, *At The Irish Exhibition Hibernia And The Grand Old Masher* (*Fun*, June 1888) the dapper old roué, Gladstone, flirts with Hibernia, the coquettish barmaid, while his jealous rival, the Tory prime minister, Lord Salisbury, observes to his nephew, Chief Secretary Balfour: 'Well, It's of no use expecting her to attend to us while he's hanging about', **Fig 31**. Lastly, Gladstone plays the role of lecher once again in Thomson's *"Comin' Thro' The Rye" or, Erin and The Grand Old Canoodler* (*Fun*, 29 October 1890). Wearing a kilt in recognition of a recent visit to his Midlothian constituency, the Liberal leader steals a kiss from demure Erin, who is holding the crozier of Home Rule, **Fig 32**.

For his part, O'Hea gave Erin the demanding role of John Bull's love interest in *"Over The Guarding Wall"* (*Weekly Freeman*, n.d.), **Fig 33**. Standing tip-toe on a ladder that leans against the wall of 'Press Misrepresentation', 'Landlords Interest', and 'Stupid Statesmanship', the portly Mr. Bull presses his case to no avail. A demanding Erin stands firmly between a love-struck Gladstone strumming his banjo of 'Household Suffrage'

Fig 32. Thomson, *"Comin' Thro' The Rye"* (*Fun*, 29 Oct. 1890)

**Fig 33**. O'Hea, *"Over the Guarding Wall"* (*Weekly Freeman*, n.d.)

and Lord Spencer on bended knee offering her a bouquet of Orange blossoms impaled by the sword of 'Vengeance For Coercion' in Reigh's *The Proud Beauty* (*United Ireland*, 17 May 1884), **Fig 34**. This cartoon played off the ongoing debate at Westminster over the third Reform Bill launched by the Liberal government that promised to extend the franchise in Ireland - a concession opposed by several Tory Members of Parliament. In *Flirting Again !!!!* (*Weekly Freeman*, 26 December 1885) O'Hea imagined Erin, empowered by the 86 seats just won by Parnellites at the general election, caught between two lecherous suitors for her affections - Gladstone and Salisbury - while a sprig of mistletoe hangs invitingly overhead. In sum, the image of courting Erin was malleable enough to contain elements of both the enchained and the empowered types. At the same time her ability to invite or repel the advances of John Bull or British ministers depended entirely on the political stance of the artist and the publisher as well as the immediate political situation.

**Fig 34**. Reigh, *The Proud Beauty* (*United Ireland*, 17 May 1884)

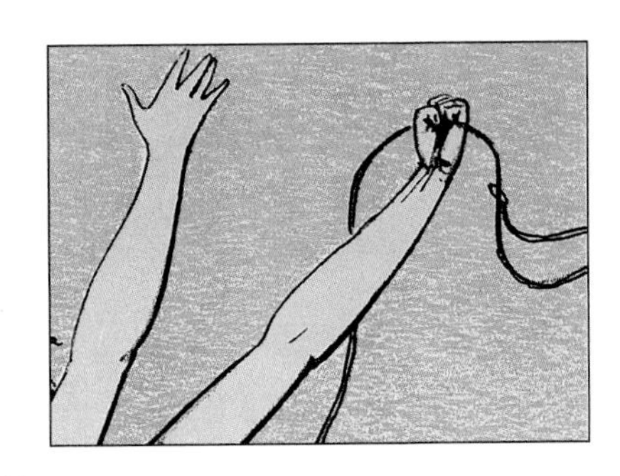

## 4. Ambiguous Erin

In the last and admittedly residual category we find an Erin who combines both the active and passive aspects of her mission to lead the Irish nation towards the promised land of Home Rule. Neither enchained nor liberated, neither conquered nor conquering, she mourns the fallen martyrs and imprisoned heroes of the nationalist struggle and summons her resources for the long campaign ahead against a formidable foe. This somewhat hybrid version owed much to the monumental and peace-loving Hibernias of the Grattanite and O'Connellite eras. Radiating sweetness and light, she grieves over the husbands, sons, and brothers who have given their lives for the cause of Irish freedom and yet she is determined to prove that they have not died in vain. No matter how mournful, she stands her ground and looks forward to the day of reckoning when John Bull will finally remove himself from her green fields. Thus, in O'Hea's *Sold Again Pat* (c.1880), she is on the verge of despair as another emigrant ship sails away, leaving her with only the Queen's Speech or Address to Parliament which is filled with empty promises.

The Phoenix Park murders in May 1882 spurred Irish cartoonists to create an Erin caught between remorse and anger. In O'Hea's *"What Villains Have Done This?"* (*Weekly Freeman*, 13 May 1882) she kneels next to the two shrouded bodies of the slain officials lying in the park. With arms upraised and eyes gazing heavenwards she seeks divine help, **Fig 35**. However, the length of rope with a noose at the end held in her left hand signifies that she is not altogether helpless at this time of crisis. O'Hea produced a more visionary Erin in *A Vision of Coming Events* (*Weekly Freeman*, 16 December 1882). With harp and wolfhound by her side she dreams of Home Rule as a vision of Parliament House emerges in the smoke rising from the fire, **Fig 36**. In the same artist's *Within Measurable Distance* (*Weekly Freeman*, 30 August 1884) Erin and her Irish-American sister (from Boston) gaze across a wide valley

**Fig 35**. O'Hea, *"What Villains Have Done This?"* (*Weekly Freeman*, 13 May 1882)

**Fig 36**. O'Hea, *A Vision of Coming Events* (*Weekly Freeman,* 16 Dec. 1882)

strewn with the rocks of coercion and landlordism at a distant acropolis symbolic of 'Legislative Independence'.

During the general election of November 1885 O'Hea depicted Erin sitting contentedly with a list of the Parnellite candidates chosen by the National League Convention. In *A Contrast* (*Weekly Freeman,* 21 November 1885), she watches a group of British politicians shouting and fighting while a kilted Gladstone plays the bagpipes. O'Hea's *Suspense !!!* (*Weekly Freeman,* 22 May 1886) portrayed her waiting expectantly outside the door of the House of Commons as M.P.s debated the fate of the first Home Rule Bill, **Fig 37**. And in *Bravo !!! Coventry* (*Weekly Freeman,* 16 July 1887) Erin takes on the risky (or risqué) role of (a fully dressed) Lady Godiva, who rides a fine white horse and holds the reins of 'Truth'. As the caption reads, 'Four Unionists go to Coventry to have a 'Peep', and they get it'. The artist leaves little to the imagination about the prurient appetite of these Peeping Tom politicians, **Fig 38**.

Even though the Parnellite split in 1890-1 caused cartoonists to produce numerous despondent Erins, they made it clear

**Fig 37**. O'Hea, *Suspense !!!* (*Weekly Freeman,* 22 May 1886)

**Fig 38**. O'Hea, *Bravo !!! Coventry* (*Weekly Freeman,* 16 July 1887)

that she would carry on the fight for freedom as well as national unity. In *"Resurgam"* (*Weekly Freeman*, 13 December 1890), conceived just after Parnell's party had broken in twain, O'Hea portrayed her weeping beneath a tree. On the ground lie two torn pieces of paper bearing in capital letters the words 'IRISH' and 'PARTY'. But Erin's harp is intact and, as the Latin title indicates, she will arise again and return to the fray, **Fig 39**. As soon as the *Freeman's Journal* decided to renounce Parnell, the cartoons in this paper became increasingly caustic about the now disgraced leader and his supporters.

The ambiguity of this model of Erin arises out of the cartoonist's emphasis on her patience, fidelity to the goal of Home Rule, and compassion for political prisoners confined by the agents of coercion. Thus, in *Erin - "You Shall Not Be Forgotten"* (*Weekly Freeman*, 6 September 1890), she wears an orange scarf, green mantle, and white dress

**Fig 39**. O'Hea, *"Resurgam"* (*Weekly Freeman*, 13 Dec. 1890)

while visiting a prison cell over which hangs a sign - 'John Kelly Four Months'. Assuring this prisoner that he will not be forgotten, she is optimistic that better days lie ahead, **Fig 40**. Unfazed by British coercion, she will resist any attempts by the British press or government to denigrate the Home Rule movement by linking it to physical force or assassination. Long accustomed to sorrows she cannot entertain thoughts of defeat.

A fine example of this Erin is *The Dawn of Freedom*, which appeared in the new anti-Parnellite newspaper, the *Weekly Freeman and National Press* (24 December 1892). Here Fitzpatrick has drawn her seated by a Celtic cross with harp and faithful wolfhound at her feet. Wearing a hopeful expression, she looks towards the rising sun and rainbow in the distance, symbolizing the sacred goal of independence, **Fig 41**.

**Fig 40.** O'Hea, *Erin - "You Shall Not Be Forgotten"* (*Weekly Freeman*, 6 Sept. 1890)

**Fig 41**. Thomas Fitzpatrick, *The Dawn of Freedom (Weekly Freeman and National Press,* 24 Dec. 1892)

# Conclusion

However selectively chosen, the cartoons discussed here should point up the diversity of roles and scenarios created by comic artists in both Dublin and London in order to convey the dynamics (and the drama) of Anglo-Irish relations during a decade of acute tension and political upheaval. Whether nationalist or unionist in their allegiance, these cartoonists were nothing if not inventive. At the same time all these widely-circulated images give rise to some awkward questions about their political and psychological impact on readers or viewers. There is so little reliable evidence about the public's response to these colour supplements that one can only indulge in speculation or conjecture. Quite apart from the obvious function of keeping the sacred flame of Irish nationalism burning brightly, these iconic figures also reinscribed the ideal of attaining a purely Irish or Gaelic nation akin to the imagined 'golden age' before the Anglo-Norman conquest.

Last but not least, we should not ignore the gender and sexual implications of beautiful and buxom Erin. Designed by male artists for a primarily, if not exclusively, male readership, this epitome of female youth and beauty must have stimulated the imaginations of ardent men in a sexually repressed society. After all, Erin was usually represented as single or unmarried - except for her partnership with or 'engagement' to Parnell. Only a handful of cartoons by O'Hea and Reigh ever assigned her the role of a mother protecting her children. And because she had none of the virago-like features of the warrior-queen Britannia, her feminine attributes had all the more appeal to men of all ages. In other words Erin - unlike 'Mother Ireland' could be sexy. Witness the feminine icons in O'Hea's *"Over the Guarding Wall"* and *Flirting Again* or Tenniel's *The Irish "Vampire"* or Thomson's series of flirtatious images in *Fun*. Combining innate nobility with peasant simplicity, she possessed endless reserves of strength as well as devotion in times of crisis. If this ideal of femininity could not compete with the pin-ups of late-twentieth-century art and photography in terms of blatant sex appeal, Erin nonetheless possessed a special allure or charm that captivated countless nationalists at the time and endures to this day.